God Put Me Back Together Piece By Piece

Table of Contents

Dedication

Dedication

I dedicate this book first and foremost to God, because without Him and the Holy Spirit living in me, there would be no book. I thank Him for seeing me through all of the heartache and keeping me.

Tony, I dedicate this book to you my deceased husband whom I love and miss. I would also like to thank your family, whom although things were rocky between us at the time of your death, I'm thankful for where we are today!

I dedicate this book to my mom, who has always been there for me, although I have taken her through many challenges. Mom, thank you for loving me no matter what. I am so thankful for our relationship today and I love you!

I would like to thank my prayer partners and sisters-in-Christ, Wendy, Jenean and Antionette. I love you ladies so much and I appreciate all of your support, encouragement and prayers.

I also would like to thank my sister, Gina; my nephew, Anthony; and my niece, Ashlee. I love you guys!

Quan, I thank you for the talk we had about what I wanted to do with my life. Our talk caused me to think about writing this book, among other things. That conversation changed my life. I love you!

I would like to thank every person who has purchased my book. Thank you for your support and I pray that God would bless you abundantly. And I can't forget you, Shantel aka Trigger, for referring me to Rachel.

Last but not least, Rachel and LaWanda. I could not have made this a book without the help of you ladies. Thank you for putting up with my attitude, temper tantrums and smart mouth at times. You turned my journal into a book and I am forever grateful for you.

Chapter 1

In the Beginning

I always wanted to have a family with two parents and I wanted my mom and dad to tell me they love me and to be there for me. My name is Patrice and I was born in Pittsburg, California. My parents, Horace and Lee got divorced when my sister and I were young; I wasn't even nine and my sister Monique was only eleven. To this day, I still don't know why they got divorced. I think I remember them arguing a lot, but it was never physical. They just couldn't get along. One day daddy moved out and we didn't see him as much. I don't know if I blocked the trauma of it out of my mind; sometimes it still hurts to think about it.

My mom worked a lot, so my sister and I were what you would now call latch key kids. We went to a Catholic School because my parents thought it would be better for us than going to a public school. When I look back at it now, I believe it was a good choice. The classes were smaller, and it was more personal, and you had that one-on-one interaction with the teacher. We went to Mass on Fridays even though we weren't Catholic. We would be home by ourselves until my mom got home which was usually around 11pm. Sometimes, I would be scared because we were both still young and if something happened, we wouldn't really be able to protect ourselves.

Our neighborhood wasn't the safest and we lived around the corner from the ghetto. You know how one area is nice with older people and then you go around the corner and there's drugs, violence, and people hanging out. We had a neighborhood store that people stood in front of doing what they do. I remember mom writing us notes to get her cigarettes only during the day but at night I felt scared because we were home alone.

It wasn't always like that; the two of us used to walk to my grandmother, Nana's house after school because she lived close to it. That was a time when I felt safe because she took care of us. Nana would take us home when my mom got off work. Once again, I can't remember the circumstances of my Nana's death just like I can't remember the circumstances of the divorce and my daddy not being at our house anymore. I was told by my mom that Nana died in her sleep. I do know that my mom was the one who found her. I don't remember a lot about Nana because I was so young when she died. As I think back, I could see her being a fast driver and active in church; I thought she was mean, me being a child, but maybe she wasn't.

After Nana's death, my sister and I had to ride the city bus to and from school. I didn't really have a lot of friends. I was shy, quiet, was never really outgoing, and I kept to myself except for hanging out with Monique. I remember playing outside and always wanting to stay out until my mom made us come inside. My mom would sometimes let me go to my friend, Nancy's, house from school because she trusted her parents. I always felt like I didn't belong and like something was missing but I didn't know what. You know you watch TV and see families that look perfect with both mom and dad there and it made me sad because I didn't have that. I would be envious of the friends I had because both of their parents lived in the home. I always wanted that. I was jealous in a way and it wasn't like my friends flaunted the fact that they had both of their parents in the home, but I just wanted my father and mother to be together.

My school served hot lunches a few days a week and I remember I had a friend, Michelle, who's mom would bring her lunch on the days when we didn't have hot lunch. Michelle would always have something from a fast-food restaurant, and I would always wish my mom would bring me lunch too. I look back now and I think I just longed for attention and I felt like maybe that was a form of love I also didn't have. I wanted my parents to hug me and to feel that love from them but I never got that. As I think back, I never understood that my mom couldn't afford it, I just thought she didn't want to give us the money and wanted us to bring our lunch because that's what she wanted. I would be so embarrassed, because all the other kids would have hot lunch when it was sold, and I would have my bag lunch.

Also, a lot of my friends' moms would pick them up from school and I would feel embarrassed, because I would have to walk to the bus stop to take the city bus home. I don't know why it bothered me so much when I saw my friends' parents together as a couple, bringing lunches, and picking them up from school; maybe because it was my desire to have something I didn't have. I'm grateful that I'm grown up and I have a better understanding. I think maybe, because I was so shy, I didn't know how to ask for what I needed or to tell them how I felt. I didn't know how to voice my feelings. Have you ever felt like if you said how you feel, it might make things worse? Well, I think that's how I felt; it was like I didn't want to say something that would make them not like me or get mad at me. I was scared. It's crazy now, because I sometimes find myself saying that kids these days tell the truth no matter what. I know it sounds strange, but after all these years, I still have this problem voicing my opinion or saying how I feel.

At the time, I didn't understand why my mom worked the hours she did and why she was never really there for us but now I understand that she had to work to pay the bills and she was struggling. But I was a child so I didn't know what I know and understand now. I remember my mom would take me and Monique with her to meet my dad at the hospital where he worked to talk. I don't know what they talked about and I remember he would make us the best french fries. They would be home-made, and he would put salt and pepper on them with ketchup on the side. To this day, whenever I make home-made fries, I think about him. It makes me sad when I think about how I never got to eat any of his other food and he was a cook.

My dad would have us every other weekend for his visitation and we would spend time with his first girlfriend, Charlene and her children and he would never really be there because he would be working. I never understood why he didn't make arrangements to be off on weekends so he could spend time with us. This was time we were supposed to be with him. I don't know why we had to go there if he wasn't going to be there. I felt like he didn't want to spend time with us. He never called to talk to us nor did he really make any effort to be with us. He was with Charlene for many years. Monique and I would go there but one of her daughters, Tina would make fun of me for being skinny and for some reason she didn't like me. I felt like Charlene was also mean to us. What did we do that would make them treat us that way? I never understood what the issue was. Was it because I was shy and quiet and didn't say much? Was it that they only wanted to treat us good when my father was around? Why wouldn't I speak up for myself? Why was I so scared? Have you ever felt like you wanted to say something but didn't know how to say it? That was me all of the time. My self-esteem kept getting lower and lower. I would cry when I was by myself, but I would never say how I felt.

In regards to my father, though he did have a father figure, I don't know if he didn't know how to be a father to me because he never had his biological father in his life. I'd ask myself, "What did I do that he pretty much didn't want anything to do with me?"

It's also a trip how now I have a friendship with Charlene's younger daughter, Sonya. She sometimes talks about my dad being a father to her. Honestly, I can't help but feel some type of way when she does. Probably because it became clear to me that he did know how to be a father. But, although I felt abandoned and rejected by my father, my heavenly Father (Jesus) was with me all the time, even though I didn't know it back then. (Psalms 27:10) says, "Even if my father and mother abandon me, the Lord will hold me close." My father entered another relationship. Tanya was her name, but I honestly can't remember the relationship with her. Monique and I became of age and were able to make decisions on the visits. We told our mom that we didn't want to go back, because he was never there so, our visits stopped. We didn't talk to our dad for almost twenty years after that. The sad part was that my dad lived in the same city as us, but we never saw him nor did he try to reach out to us. I didn't understand why he didn't reach out. We always had the same number and lived in the same house until years later when mom moved us to another city.

My mom was very close to her younger sister, Matilda. We would go to her house to visit often. We also had a neighbor, Jerome, who was a drug addict and alcoholic but was considered family. He visited Matilda's house too. One day I was trying to take a nap and Jerome came and sat on the couch where I was laying. He started fondling me. My face was laying toward the inside of the couch, so we weren't facing each other, but I felt his fingers touching my vagina on the outside of my pants. This lasted for about two to three minutes. I just laid there in shock, scared and didn't know what to do. I froze and couldn't move. I was paralyzed with fear. Then it stopped! Afterwards,

I turned over to see who it was and it was Jerome! It bothered me so much that I got sick to my stomach and started vomiting. I thought, "Why would this man do this to me? We never had any type of relationship or talks, because he was a grown man. Not to mention, friends with my mom. Did he do it because I was shy and quiet and he preyed on me because of that?" I was young and I had never had any kind of sexual experiences before. I felt violated and dirty.

I also, blamed myself. I felt maybe I should not have had my backside towards the outside of the couch. So why wouldn't I say anything when he was doing this, why didn't I scream, or yell or try to get away! Patrice, what was wrong with you? Why didn't I get up right away after it happened and tell my mom and aunt?

Later as I got older, I realized, I couldn't blame myself for what Jerome did to me. I was a child and I was innocent. He was sick and needed help. There was nothing I did wrong nor did I do anything to deserve what he did to me. But at that time, I just wanted to keep myself safe. Hopefully, he didn't do this to some other young child.

I don't know if this has ever happened you, who's reading this, but the experience is like you don't know what to do. You can't move or do anything when it's happening and you're stuck. I hear about predators preying on children that are quiet and keep to themselves.

I guess my mom and aunt could see I was a little withdrawn and started asking me if I was ok and why my stomach was so upset. I finally told them what happened. They cussed Jerome out and kicked him out the house. But no charges were ever filed. I guess back in those days, families hid those type of things under the rug. Needless to say, we never talked to him again. Both my mom and aunt told me never to be afraid to tell them if something like this happened. I never had counseling or anything after that, but now I know that my mom should've taken me to talk to someone. But again, back then the belief was, "What goes on in this house, stays in this house.". However, I did feel better after telling them what happened. It made me feel safe and all of my fears did go away. Although my mom didn't press charges or take any farther actions, I felt like someone was finally on my side. They defended me, didn't blame me or made me feel that it was my fault.

It is never the victim's fault when someone assaults them. Even when you do nothing to stop it.

Chapter 2

Struggling to Fit In

After my grandmother on my mom's side passed away, my mom and some of her siblings stopped talking because they were fighting over her belongings. She remained close to one of her sisters, Matilda, her brother Jeff, and his wife, Donna. We would go to my Uncle Jeff's house a lot. It would be so much fun because my cousin was a little older so he would take us on rides in his car or we would just hang out with him. Uncle Jeff's wife, Donna had a brother named Lloyd and he and my mom started dating. They were in a serious relationship and he would come over a lot. He was like a father to my sister and I. We loved him and loved when he came over. We moved in with Lloyd in Fairfield, California. I left my hometown and now lived in a new city. I was scared and nervous because not only was I leaving familiar places and faces, I would have to start a new school. A public school, instead of the private school I was used to. So, no more uniforms and no more one classroom. I also, had to make new friends. I was not happy, but I had no choice. I was pretty much starting all over in a foreign place. At the same time though, I was happy, because we got to live with Lloyd. I longed for so long to feel like a complete family. In the back of my mind, starting a new school made me ask myself, "How am I going to do this when I'm shy, skinny and not sociable?" I didn't just go up to people and start talking. But, I started the new school and I did make a few friends. Sometimes God takes us out of what is familiar to us and places us in a new environment so we can grow.

I can't remember what was going on, but there was something at school and they had a pie eating contest. I don't remember why or how I entered it. I'm eating the pie and I hear for the first time ever in my life, something like, look at Patrice with those big lips. I don't think it would have ever bothered me if everyone hadn't laughed. I was so embarrassed. Even though I was almost a teenager, I never thought about that part of my body as being ugly until someone said something and it made people laugh. I know you all have heard the saying, "Sticks and stones may break my bones, but words will never hurt me." Well, this is a lie from the pit of hell. People don't realize that the words they say can hurt and stay with people for years. I got through the contest and all I wanted to do was go home. I went home and all I could do was cry.

Sadly, I felt like I could never talk to my mom about my feelings, because she never made me feel like I could. Even though she said I could tell her when something was wrong after the incident with Jerome, she was never the type of mom that would say comforting or encouraging words. She would be negative and I never felt encouraged when I talked to her. Her daily routine was work, come home, watch TV and repeat! She was just unapproachable. (Psalm 139:14) says, "I will praise you for I am fearfully and wonderfully made."

Having luscious lips was never an issue or ever brought to my attention until that day. Now it's 2020 and women are paying to get their lips injected and I have them naturally. God made me with these lips and He doesn't make any mistakes. I'm made in His image. I discovered this on my own.

Unfortunately, my mom's relationship with Lloyd didn't last long. So here we are moving again and having to change schools again. I'm not sure what happened between the two of them except that they didn't get along. Lloyd would come to our new house sometimes, but we didn't see him as much and eventually he just stopped coming altogether. Surprisingly, it didn't really affect me as it should have. Most likely, because I was older and I felt at peace. Or maybe, because I didn't have to deal with those kids who made fun of my lips. Yet still, I had to adjust again to a new school and new kids. This time, I had to ride the school bus. I already had a hard time during middle school (7th and part of 8th grade). But now I had to try and adjust to this new environment and make new friends again. I made some friends but I was still shy. I still had a hard time gaining weight (that's a whole other subject) and I just felt out of place. I couldn't get the comments about my lips out of my head. After that comment, I started really dealing with low self-esteem and I didn't like anything about myself. In addition, although my mom worked, she didn't really buy me clothes. So, I felt I didn't fit in, because other kids had nice clothes and I didn't. I didn't realize it at the time, although my mom worked hard, she just couldn't afford it. I was a teenager and all I knew was that I wanted better clothes and she wouldn't buy them for me.

I eventually put what Jerome did to me in the back of my mind and didn't think about it. However, I was still having a hard time emotionally, physically, mentally and socially. I don't know what was happening to me and didn't understand my feelings.

I remember having my first crush on a boy, but I would never tell him. We would talk as friends and it never went past that. I was too shy to tell him and I didn't know if I would be rejected. If he did reject me, I don't think I could've handled it. Then there was a boy on the bus who started making fun of my lips, so once again, I'm dealing with the humiliation while everyone laughed. I was so shy that I would just sit there and not say anything. Low self-esteem was kicked up another 1000 notches. I felt so low. The embarrassment came back, and I felt like I was going backwards and not forward. I didn't think I would have to deal with this again. I felt so ugly! I couldn't help wondering, "Is this what my life is going to be like forever? If so, I just can't deal with this!" I needed to find a way to get rid of this pain, because it was too much for me and I didn't have anyone to talk to. I didn't think anyone would understand because the people who were in my life didn't look like me and I always felt like I was the ugly one in the family. It was not long after, that I just decided that I didn't want to live anymore. I was at home feeling so low, I decided to take some pills hoping I would just go to sleep and not wake up. I got so sick and started vomiting.

At first, I didn't tell my mom, but I got scared because I didn't know what was going to happen. When I did tell her, she got mad because she had to take me to the ER. The doctor checked me out, and said I was ok, it just had to run its course. I was sent home and I never got counseling or any help for that situation. However, the doctor never suggested it either. My mom yelled at me and asked why I did it. She was never the type of mother who really showed me love. We never said, "I love you" nor did we ever hug or show any type of affection towards each other.

Even after the suicide attempt, my mom continued with her daily routine and I still couldn't talk to her. So, I continued to just keep everything to myself. Looking back, I was too young to consider that maybe she only gave me what was given to her by my grandmother. I don't know what my mother's relationship was like with her mom, because I was young when my grandmother died. But I don't remember them ever saying, "I love you" to each other. Today, I can't help feeling like I still needed her to be my mom. I know what I did was wrong, but I feel like she could have at least hugged me, told me she loved me and that it would all be ok. Maybe you, who's reading my story, may have gone through something like this and still feel an empty void. Let me tell you, you're not alone. I thank God for Jesus.

He filled that void for me and he will do it for you.

But again, how could my mom give what she didn't have in her to give. However, I was a child unable to understand. I got through that situation and made it through my 8th grade graduation. But God!! He had a plan for me, even though I didn't know it at the time: It wasn't my time to die and God had so much in store for me and He was just getting started. Although I would have to go through more things, He was with me through it all and I didn't even know Him yet!! It says in (Jeremiah 29:11), "For I know the thoughts that I think toward you, says the Lord, thoughts of peace and not of evil, to give you a future and a hope."

Freshman year, I thought this year would be good because my sister, Monique and friends who were more like family, Wendy and Rhonda, attended the same school. Monique and Wendy were the same age, and Rhonda and I were the same age. But that low self-esteem continued to pop up. I always thought Rhonda was so pretty and I admit, I was a little jealous of her because she always had confidence. You could see she was happy with herself. Also, the guys liked her and they had no problem letting it be known. I would think to myself, "What's wrong with me and why don't people find me attractive?" I even questioned God, "Why did you make me like this?"

Monique and I would go to Wendy and Rhonda's house and our families became really close. But, I always felt like the ugly one in the group. Everyone was pretty, but me. I was still skinny and not able to gain weight. Their dad was like a dad to us. I even started calling him daddy and he was ok with that. I envied Wendy and Rhonda, because they had both of their parents in the home. Their mom worked at a store and she would bring them clothes or pretty gifts. I wished my mom would have done that for us. They had things that my mom couldn't afford to give Monique and I. It was especially hard around Christmas time, because my mom couldn't afford to get me things I wanted. But I was a teenager, and I didn't realize that she just couldn't afford it. She did the best she could and I don't think my father was helping her. The fact that I wasn't able to wear nice clothes like other kids bothered me because I already felt ugly and when you don't feel good about how you're dressed or how your hair looks, it makes it worse. Some of you readers may know what I'm talking about.

Even when people would talk to me, I always felt like it was because I was with Monique, Wendy and Rhonda. At my high school, classrooms were in buildings that were divided into sections. So, some classes you had to walk quite a ways to get to. One of the buildings was called the Annex. I hated having classes in the Annex, because you had to walk past this area that smelled like animals and it stunk so bad. So, one day I was walking to the annex, mustering through the stench of animals, to get to class. But the teacher wasn't there yet, so I stood outside. One of my classmates walked up to me and said, "You probably already know what I'm going to say. Patrice you have big lips. Why are your lips so big?" I was hurt and embarrassed, but I didn't say anything. I just ignored it. I don't have to tell you that it bothered me. It definitely added fuel to my low self-esteem fire. Why was everyone so focused on my lips? But I was a teenager and didn't have the understanding that I have now. I also didn't have a relationship with God nor did I know that the bible says, "God made man in His image." (Genesis 1:27). I didn't know His word to realize that God made me and He makes no mistakes. God made you and I just the way we are for a reason. He made us this way because He wanted to. If everyone looked the same, the world would be a boring place.

I was still shy and only felt confident around Wendy, Rhonda, and Monique. I loved being around Wendy and Rhonda and their family because they always had fun and they spent time together as a family. I longed for that! There was an emptiness in my heart, and I didn't' know how to fill it. I knew something was missing but it took me years to find it and figure out what it was. Now, I know it was God!! My mom was also strict, and she would say no a lot when I wanted to do something. I always felt like she wanted me to stay in the house. Wendy, Rhonda, Monique, and I, the crew, would go to football games and then hang out afterwards. My mom always wanted us in the house earlier than everyone else. I made it through the first two years of high school and by then Monique and Wendy graduated I was a junior and more comfortable in school, although it was just me and Rhonda.

A few years had passed and I had adjusted to being more outgoing. It was Halloween, the crew and a few other friends, except Monique wanted to go to a party at the Party Palace. Of course, my mom didn't want us to go and Wendy and Rhonda's mom, Vera didn't want us to go either. Vera would sometimes say she had a feeling something was going to happen, but we always thought she just said that because she didn't want us to go anywhere. They finally gave in and let us go, so we drove in our friend, Wanita's car. We were so happy because we were able to go out and have fun which meant drinking and partying. That was the plan. Wanita didn't drink so she was the designated driver. The last thing I remember was going to McDonalds and getting on Air Base Parkway. I woke up in the hospital being wheeled in a bed and being asked if I knew where I was. I learned that we were almost at the party, Wanita turned at the green light and a drunk driver ran the light and hit us. Everyone made it out ok, but they had to get me out with the jaws of life. It took a while before I was comfortable riding in a car again. To this day, I still don't remember the accident and I'm glad because that's something I wouldn't want to relive. I just know, God was there with me even when I didn't know Him. They saw it as the Jaws of Life, but it was the Grace of God, who saved me.

I got a job working at McDonalds after school. It felt good because I was making my own money and was able to buy clothes and some of the things my mom couldn't afford. I finally felt like I was growing up and becoming an adult. Rhonda and I had a friend, Susan, who had a car. We would make up any reason to use her car, even tell lies. We would say we had to go to our house for some reason or wanted to get something to eat. She'd let us go and we would be gone until school was out; just in time to pick her up. We would go everywhere, including, driving to a totally different city to hang out with older friends.

I enjoyed hanging out with older people when I was a teenager. I would drink and smoke weed with them. When I drank it gave me confidence and the shyness went away. They say alcohol is like liquid courage. The guys we hung out with had a house and we would go there. Some of them would try to get at me, but I wasn't interested. I was just there for the weed and alcohol. I never had a relationship with any of them. It was mostly just friendship, but we always had fun. Most of them sold drugs and I just loved being around that lifestyle. I loved how they always had money and didn't have to work a 9 to 5 job. It was crazy that I was never afraid of anything bad happening when I was around them. I never thought about having a career or doing anything with my life other than making sure I was able to take care of myself. Besides graduating from high school, my mom never encouraged me to go to college to have a career, so that's all I strived for. She always told me to make sure you can pay your bills and keep a roof over your head. I never pushed myself to do anything better beyond high school. Sometimes, I wish I could go back to my senior year and do it all over again. I would do things so different now. But that's the thing about wisdom, its accumulated after going through. Anyways, I graduated and got my diploma. My mom gave me a nice graduation party.

Unfortunately, graduating high school didn't change my mind-set of living for the moment. I quit my job, because I just wanted to hang out. Wendy and I had these friends who were sisters, Alicia and Myra, and we would go to their house because their mom would let us do whatever we wanted, even drink. So of course, we always wanted to go there. That house was the party house and I was the party girl. I had no idea what I wanted to do with myself. I was literally existing day by day with no thought of the future. I was living with my mom, doing nothing just hanging out. After a while, that got old and I tried going to the local college. But that didn't last long either, because I got bored with it. I had jobs here and there but I would get tired of them and quit. I believe during this time, I just wanted to make easy money. I didn't want to put in the time nor the effort. Most of all, I didn't want to work a full-time job. I had no idea what I wanted to do with myself, but I knew something had to change.

So, remember I told you about the guys I hung around with who sold drugs? That life they lived looked so fun because they didn't work a 9-5 job and they were making easy money? Well, I became really close with one of them, TJ, and we started hanging out all the time. We were like brother and sister. I went everywhere with him. I would go with him to pick up his drugs, to cook the dope and to deliver it. After a while, I started keeping it at my house, well my mom's house. Dealers would come to me and pick it up. I would weigh it and make sure it was good and give it to them. TJ was cheap, but he always made sure I was taken care of. Surprisingly, we never thought of being together in a romantic way and even more surprising, he ended up dating Wendy for a while. I never thought about getting caught by the police or getting robbed or killed. Sadly, other dealers were getting robbed, set up and killed all the time. I think I liked the rush or the thrill of it. It was fun to me. TJ was well known in his city and I was well known for hanging around him. I had no idea that my decisions had consequences and how they would affect my life. I was getting ready to do some things that would alter my life forever.

Chapter 3

Did I Really Do That

I decided to start selling dope. I would weigh and bag TJ's drugs. His clients started getting the dope from me and I would skim some off the top to keep for myself to sell. I saw how easy it was to make that fast money. For example, you could sell a rock and get $20 in less than an hour or in just a few minutes. I don't remember how I got my customers, but I did. I had a loyal customer named Tommy and I would go sit at his house. His friends were dope fiends who would come and would buy drugs from me. I treated selling dope like it was a real job, just with no retirement plan. Like I said before, I didn't think about going to jail, getting robbed or killed. I liked the thrill of it and the fact that I was in control, because people on drugs will do whatever you say to get that next high. There would be times when I came close to getting caught with dope on me. One night I was at a dope fiend's house who was on probation. I was there with drugs on me, but I put the dope in my bra and they weren't able to search me. They never could find any dope in the house.

Another time I was driving to the dope track and right when I was getting ready to turn into the parking lot, I saw all of these police cars at Tommy's house. Yes, it was being raided.

I can't help, but to stop and give God the praise. He kept me in the mist of my mess. Although there were other dope dealers around, I was Tommy's only supplier. I would give drugs on credit, because I knew the paydays of certain dope fiends. I also took food stamps. When I think back to how I took food stamps from some of them, I feel bad because they had kids. I took food out of those kid's mouth. I hate that I did that, especially, because of how I felt about my mom not being able to give me some of the things I wanted. Those poor kids couldn't help that their parents were on drugs and I didn't help the situation by taking the food stamps as payment. I was selfish, but I was a hustler and in "hustler mode".

I reconnected with one of my cousins, Jeff Jr., my uncle's son. I didn't realize at the time that Jeff Jr. was addicted to crack. He introduced me to some people who used dope, so I started selling to them. I got more clientele. I also sold to him. He was living with his girlfriend at the time and they had a young daughter. I know it's bad to sell drugs to your family members, but I never thought about that. I feel bad now, but I didn't back then because it was all about money for me. I was still living with my mom and I don't think she ever knew about what I did or if she did, she never said anything. She was still working a lot, so I didn't see her much.

Unlike most drug dealers, I wasn't big time. I just did it to survive. The crazy thing is, I thought the money was good enough to where I didn't think about how I was wasting my life or about my future. I thank God that he never allowed me to try crack, because I don't know if I would have become addicted. I saw how some of the people I sold to would act and I never wanted to experience that. One lady would get in a fetal position on her couch and say she was hearing things when high. That in itself made me not want to ever try crack.

I had one client named Vanisha and we actually became friends. She was a "smoker" (a person who smokes drugs from a pipe), but she would work and take care of herself. She always kept a place to stay and she liked nice things. She was kind of bougie, but she liked to get high. She would only date men who took care of her and had been in a long-time relationship with a married man. He was paying for her to live in a nice apartment. TJ and I would go to her house and hang out where she would let him cook his dope. That's actually how I learned how to cook dope for the first time. Vanisha and the married guy broke up and she had to learn how to survive on her own. She ended up getting into another relationship with this much older man who put her up in a house. I would go hang out there when I wasn't at Tommy's house.

During this time, although I was living with my mom, all I would do is go home, shower, change my clothes and go back out. One day I came home and my mom sat me down and said that she thought it would be better if I moved out, because I was treating her home like a motel. So, although I was kind of hurt in a way, I was actually ok with it. I talked to Vanisha and she let me stay with her. You know the saying , "The grass isn't always greener on the other side." This is so true. After I moved in with Vanisha I felt like the men she would date. She wanted me to pay for this and pay for that plus give her free dope. I was doing all that I could and I was hardly there because I was always at Tommy's house selling drugs. Needless to say, this arrange-ment didn't last long and there I was asking my mom if I could move back in. I didn't want my mom to kick me out again, so I got a job but would still sell dope on the side. However, I ended up quitting my job and went back to selling dope full-time. This time, though, I had a plan. I didn't hang out so much so my mom wouldn't notice and kick me out again.

It's funny how time passes, because as I got older, I realized I needed to do something with myself. Besides that, my clientele was decreasing. Decreased clientele, also meant a decrease in the flow of money. I just didn't know what I wanted to do or where to start. I was older, and I hadn't really thought about my future career. I didn't know what direction my life was heading in. But one thing I did know for sure was that hanging out, drinking and selling dope was not the life I wanted to live anymore.

I was still hanging with Tommy and one day we went to the store. We saw a dope dealer that Tommy knew named Tony, whom everyone called REV. He asked who I was and Tommy introduced us. Tony gave me his pager number. This is where the pieces of me started falling....

Chapter 4

Relationship and Heartache

Tony and I started talking and spending time together. But it wasn't really anything serious, because he was doing his thing and so was I. We both were focused on making money. I was in my early 20's and had never really had a relationship with anyone. I had acquaintances and had sexual encounters, but I never had anything really serious to where I can say I was ever in love. Tony was living with his mom, like I was, and his son was two years old at the time. I didn't realize that he was still kind of seeing his son's mom at the time. We were still just occasionally seeing each other and it wasn't serious. But I loved spending time and talking on the phone with him.

I fell hard for Tony, but I didn't want to tell him, because I wanted to protect my heart. Plus, I didn't want to get rejected. He was the first person I ever really had feelings for in that way. I didn't want to hear him say that he didn't want to be in a relationship with me.

I wouldn't call him much and one time I let a week go by without reaching out to him. He called, and asked "Why haven't you called me?" I said, "I didn't want to seem needy or desperate." He said, "I like you and want to get to know you better." He also said he was still struggling with his relationship with his son's mother and I said ok. I was glad I didn't tell him how I really felt. We didn't see much of each other, so I just kept it moving with my life, selling dope, and doing me! I thought about him a lot, but still didn't tell him how I felt.

I didn't have a lot of friends and by this time, everyone I knew had kids of their own. Wendy and Rhonda both had a child. Monique was married and had my niece and nephew, but by this time, she was separated and in a relationship with someone else. They were all doing their own thing. I was the only one in the crew who didn't have a child. I was also, never one to deal with my hurt. I would always try to be strong and just keep it moving. I might cry for a minute, but I'd just move on.

Whoever is reading this, please don't ever push your feelings to the side. Deal with them by either talking to someone you trust, go to counseling and/or write in a journal. It will help you when you're struggling with pain on the inside. Anyways, as I said, Tony and I didn't talk that much. I realized he was in a committed relationship with his son's mom. I couldn't get mad, because it's not like we were in a relationship. But it did hurt. I told myself, "Okay Patrice, it's time to move on." One day, things just changed between us and he called me out of the blue and took me out on a date. We went to dinner in the Bay Area and then to the Berkeley Marina. We walked and talked. This was the beginning of what I thought would be a beautiful relationship.

We started spending a lot of time together but he went to jail, because of driving tickets. He wanted me to spend time with his mom and get to know her. It felt nice getting to know his mom, MaeD, because she was all about family. He left me his Camaro to use and gave me his pager to use to make more money. I think he didn't want me out in the streets while he was gone, but he did want me to make money. Tony finally got out and we were together all the time.

I got a full-time job and I finally weened myself from selling dope. Tony also didn't want me selling dope anymore, but I didn't do it for him; I did it for me. I really liked my new job at the Thrift store as a retail worker and I loved my schedule. I would go to work, go home to shower, get dressed, and go spend the night with Tony. I was so comfortable at his mom's house, because she always made me feel like that was my home. Tony's mom had taken custody of a close family friend's daughter and we were constantly watching her while MaeD and her boyfriend went out. MaeD also had two mentally delayed sons that we would watch.

Tony was still selling dope, but I didn't mind watching the kids while he made runs. I loved feeling like I was part of a real family, because this was like a dream come true. I felt like things in my life were good, but you know what they say, "All good things must come to an end." Tony and I had a sexual relationship, but I never got pregnant. I was still young and I never thought about it. There was a time when I was a week late for my period and I thought I might be pregnant. I went to the doctor and the test came back negative. I was disappointed, but I eventually got over it. I just felt it wasn't my time yet. I always felt special when I was with Tony. He spoiled me. He would cook for me and give me anything I wanted. I never had to worry about spending my money because he took care of everything. I thought we were going to get married. He would show me through his actions that he loved me and wanted to be with me at that time. We would talk about our future and went to his family functions together. Tony had a big family, so I was always meeting someone new. He would come to my job sometimes and we would go to lunch. When I was with him, I didn't think about my low self-esteem or feel bad about myself in any way.

One day, Tony came to my job dressed differently than he normally did, with his friend Steve. I asked him where he was going, and he said nowhere. I didn't think anything else about it. That was the beginning of Tony acting different and becoming distant. He went from being at his mom's house with me to hardly being there while I was there. At first, I just figured he was hanging out making money or with Steve. Then it became more frequent and I would go to sleep at MaeD's house and he wouldn't be there. I didn't know what was going on. So, there I was questioning myself. "Did I do something wrong and he just didn't say anything?" I wondered, "Is he not attracted to me anymore or does he just not want to be with me anymore?" The self-loathing resurfaced. I eventually stopped going to MaeD's house and just started going home from work.

After a few days, I asked Tony to come by so we could talk. It was awkward, because he didn't even come in the house. He just came to the door and talked to me through a partially open screen door. I can't remember exactly what was said, but it came down to him saying something like he wanted to be with me, but not in a serious relationship. He said we would still spend time together and talk, but when he closed that door, I knew it was over. He just wasn't man enough to tell me. I would reach out to him and sometimes he would answer and sometimes he wouldn't. The times we did talk, it was still awkward, short, and he wouldn't really say anything. A lot of the times it was dead silence on the phone and I could tell he didn't want to talk to me. I was devastated because, this was someone whom I thought wanted to marry me and be with me forever. I still didn't understand what happened. Eventually the calls stopped, but I just wanted to know what happened.

I still had a really good relationship with MaeD. She knew I was hurting, so one day she told me to come over and I did. We were in her room talking and she was sorting through clothes. I just straight out asked her if Tony was seeing someone else and she said yes. MaeD said that she wasn't going to lie to me about it. I asked her if the girl was nice and if she liked her. MaeD answered yes to both, but what I didn't realize was that I knew who she was. It was a close family friend, Meeka, who had been at MaeD's house a lot. She was actually like a part of their family. I felt sick and then I just got mad. I was mad because Meeka was in my face talking to me and behind my back messing with my man. That's why I never liked dealing with women and didn't trust them. Most of all, because I always felt as though women were messy and would go behind your back like Meeka. I left MaeD's house heartbroken again after hearing the news. But deep down inside, I already knew in my heart that he was seeing someone else. I just didn't want to believe it.

I went home and my mom asked what was wrong. I told her what happened and she said if he doesn't want to be with you it's his loss and I deserved better. But I couldn't see that at the time. It felt good to hear mom say that to me and hug me. For the first time, I felt like my mom cared about me. Unfortunately, it wasn't enough to stop the pain. All I knew was I just got hurt by the first person I ever truly loved and I didn't know how I was going to get through it. I just wanted to scream! I was so mad that all I could think of was, how could I hurt him as much as he's hurt me? I even drove to his house to slash his tires, but I ended up going home because I knew he would have known it was me. I didn't want to go through the possibility of being accused of it. Naw, let's just face it. I got scared and didn't know what he would do if I had done that. Not that he ever hurt me physically before, but I just didn't want to take any chances or suffer the consequences.

I couldn't eat or sleep. All I did was go to work and come home. I didn't want to go anywhere or do anything. I barely wanted to get out of the bed. I lost so much weight that I looked like I was on crack, because I was so skinny. I just looked sick or unlike myself. It's almost indescribable how you can look in the mirror and not be able to recognize yourself.

I was so depressed that I even thought about suicide again, because I just didn't want to hurt anymore. The low self-esteem returned. I started questioning myself, what was wrong with me? I really wanted this relationship to work. I thought he loved me. How could he hurt me like this? I just didn't know what to do with these feelings I had. But there was a lady I worked with at McDonalds when I was in high school. I didn't remember her, but she would come to my job a lot and always invite me to go to church. I kept telling her no. I didn't realize that my life was about to change. God was drawing me to Him and I didn't even know it yet. He was getting ready to show me how much He loves me more than any man ever could.

So, I finally said yes to First Lady M and I went to church. I just cried and cried. I know the Holy Spirit led me and I ended up giving my life to the Lord!!

Chapter 5

Salvation and Healing

I felt like a weight had been lifted from me. I felt this peace that I had never experienced before. First Lady M would always check on me. She would pray with me and it didn't matter what time of the day or night it was. I went to church every Sunday and I felt safe there, because I always felt God's presence. After church, I would go home and the pain and hurt would come back again. I still struggled with my feelings for Tony and I knew it was because there was no closure. When I had those feelings, I prayed, read my Bible and cried out to God. As time went on, I didn't cry anymore. I didn't know what happened or what made him go to someone else, but I accepted it. It was hard getting over him! All I could do was just take it day by day.

I got involved in the different ministries at the church and I was there anytime the doors were open. I would serve wherever there was a need. The church became my life and it was a way to escape my pain. When I served others, I wasn't thinking of Tony and the pain he caused me. However, I was still lonely and I missed our relationship. I missed the love, attention, affection and affirmation he would give me daily. I didn't think I would ever find someone who would make me feel like that again. We lived in a small town, but I never saw him when I went out. I believe God did that, because He knew my heart wasn't ready to see him. I also believe God knew that I was still willing to take Tony back if he'd asked me to.

I know now that it wasn't our time. I had to go through that hard break up. I believe God used that heartache to draw me to Him. God knew He had to do something drastic to get me to surrender to Him. The lifestyle I lived, God protected me, while I still did my own thing. If He hadn't taken me through that hurt, I wouldn't have come to Him. The pain slowly went away and I wasn't thinking about Tony like I used to. But, I never stopped praying for him and his salvation. I didn't date because there were no men asking me out. I wondered what was going on and if God was going to bless me with a husband. There was no one in the church and the ones who were there, I wasn't interested in. So, I just kept my focus on God and my relationship with Him.

By this time, I hadn't talked to my dad in years, but my mom told me she heard he had throat cancer. She said he was doing good and it wasn't life threatening at that time. I didn't reach out to him, but I was happy that he was ok. Since I never had a relationship with him, I didn't see the need to call him. I was still living with my mom and had come to terms with the fact that I would be with her until marriage. That was if I ever got married.

One day, my dad called me and Monique out of the blue apologizing for not being there and not having a relationship with us. He asked for our forgiveness and of course we said yes. My dad said his cancer had progressed and he wasn't doing well. I knew he meant that he was dying. He was living in San Diego with my Aunt Ida, his sister who was a registered nurse. She was taking care of him. I asked if Monique and I could come see him and he said he didn't think it would be a good idea. This is where I learned that he was in a relationship with someone named Anita and they had a son, Kevin. Yes, I had a brother whom I had never met. My feelings were hurt because he didn't want us to come see him because of Anita. He said he didn't want to cause problems. I let it go because he was sick. "But daddy, once again you're rejecting me and Monique for someone else." Yes, it was his biological son. But we were his biological kids too. I cried, but once again there was nothing I could do. I bottled up my feelings and put them aside for the sake of someone else, yet again. All these thoughts kept coming up like, "Daddy, you have a son who's been with you longer than you've ever been with me and Monique." I was mad, felt rejected, and angry thinking, "Here we go again, someone else rather than us."

A week later, Monique and I got the call from Aunt Ida that our daddy was gone; he died! She said he was in so much pain, it hurt just for her to bathe him. One of the things I truly thank God for is that when I had that last conversation with my daddy, I asked him if he had confessed Jesus Christ as his personal Lord and Savior and he said yes!!! Thank you Jesus, because I know that my daddy is with the Lord!! Monique and I flew to Florida for the funeral. When we got there, we saw a lot of family members that we hadn't seen in years. We also met family for the first time. I didn't cry until the funeral. It had been fifteen years since I had seen my daddy. Seeing him made me break down. Anita and Kevin weren't there and I didn't know why. Many years later I would meet them for the first time.

We got through the funeral and returned to California to our normal lives. Monique cried, but she never spoke about her feelings. In general, it's hard to get Monique to talk about her feelings. I only felt fulfilled and happy when I was praying. I had a hard time telling people no so when I was asked to do something I would say yes even if I didn't want to do it. I also felt like I had to say yes, because I was now a Christian and thought, "What Would Jesus Do?" I was taught that you have to obey your Pastors and that's what I was doing no matter what. Mom would get mad and say I'm spending too much time at the church. I don't know why she had a hard time with me being at church. At least I wasn't in the street selling dope or hanging out drinking, right? I just prayed and kept it moving. What else could I do? Besides, I finally had something in my life that was helping me deal with the pain of my break up with Tony and finding myself. I loved to pray for people and myself. I felt close to God and it made me feel good inside. I can't describe the feeling, but I didn't want it to end.

I made some beautiful friendships at church. I was a part of many weddings and I loved seeing people happy. I can't lie, I wanted marriage, too, and I was in my mid-twenties. It would be Wendy, Rhonda, and me. Yes, the crew, except for Monique, had become Christians and we were all part of the same church. People called us the three musketeers, because we were single and hung out together, and being a part of all these ministries. We were also called the faithful few, because we were doing a lot in the church. Me and the crew would get teased because everyone else was getting married and the fact that we were still single. I was wondering what was wrong with me and why was it taking so long for my husband to find me? I was getting older and my biological clock was ticking. I felt like my time was running out. Everyone else was passing me by and it seemed like time had stopped for me. I had gotten to the point where I was over Tony and the hurt, but now, I was dealing with loneliness and wondering when it would be my turn for true love.

Chapter 6

God's Work

One of the ministries that the crew and I were thrown into was ushering. An Elder at the church called us each by name and told us we were now ushers. I didn't know anything about being an usher, but I learned. Wendy was Head Usher and God had given her so much creativity and insight on how to run it. We also learned how to discern the different spirits operating in the church. God was teaching me things through that season and I am grateful. I believe my healing came through being at church because I was serving. I did everything my Pastors told me to do. I never questioned them and I believed everything they said. I was committed, but I was also a little naïve. I thought, "Your Pastors would never lie or steer you wrong, would they?" One thing I do appreciate them for, is that they pushed me to use my gifts and talents for the Kingdom. We were an outreach ministry, so we would go out and give tracs regarding salvation and feed the homeless once a month. One day, Pastor M came to my apartment, which he and First Lady M were managers of. I was reading my notes from Sunday's service. He looked at them and said he wanted me to teach bible study that following Wednesday. My stomach got sick all of a sudden and I was nervous. I have always had a hard time speaking in front of people. I said ok, but I was nervous and had butterflies in my stomach that whole week. Public speaking is hard for me. I love being in the background. With prayer, I always felt like I was in my element and I loved it. God would sometimes speak to me and tell me what to pray for people or He would have me say something to someone.

Anyway, I was no longer working at the Thrift Store and was unemployed. I was heavily involved in church. Pastor M put me over the Prayer Ministry and I had noon prayer Monday through Friday. Most of the time it was just me or Pastor M would have me pick him up and he would do things at the church while I prayed. There was something about that alone time with God at the altar that fulfilled me. I was having a hard time finding a job, but I kept trusting God which was all I could do. Can you imagine a once upon a time drug dealer, making easy money to now being on unemployment and having just enough to give tithes and pay the little bills? God took care of me and He met my every need. (Phil: 4:19), "But my God shall supply all of your need according to his riches in glory by Christ Jesus." And that

He did!

Feeding the homeless was another ministry that was close to my heart. I always felt that could've been me if my mom had not let me live with her. I would have been homeless trying to figure out where I would get my next meal or lay my head. But God!! The homeless need love and to know that someone cares for them. So, I guess I saw myself in each of them. I would find any reason to bless my Pastor and First Lady M, who was also a Pastor. If I had extra money or if there was something I could do for them, I would bless them. I believed that is what I was supposed to do, because they were my shepherds, and I made a commitment to help take care of them. People would come and go at the church and when they left, the Pastors would always say that person had an issue with the ministry. They always made it seem like the people who left had a problem and of course I believed them.

This church was my first ministry and I was focused on my relationship with God and growing closer to Him. I was growing spiritually and I was content with my life. I was getting tired of saying yes, all the time, but I felt guilty if I said no. I was doing so much and I was worn out. I thought I would make God mad if I said no, especially to my Pastors. There would be people in church that would ask me to do things and I felt like I was being taken advantage of. I still wouldn't say anything. Once again, I would hold it inside and not voice my feelings. I just didn't want the confrontation.

There was a time I loaned someone money and they never paid me back. I was so mad about it! I went to Pastor M and he said I have to release that person. I had a hard time at first, because I would see this person buying clothes for their children and taking trips. One day I went to the person and told her I released her from her debt. She said she was going to come to me about making payment arrangements. You can imagine what I was thinking, but I just told her no, she's released. I had to let it go and that's what I did. Things were going well in my life, but I had no idea that things were about to change and something unimaginable was about to happen. I would lose yet another piece of myself...

Chapter 7

We Meet Again/Second Chances

I always sent MaeD a Mother's Day card, even after Tony and I had broken up. And she would always call me to thank me. One year she called me and asked how I was doing. We caught up with each other. She asked me to hold on and the next thing I knew she had Tony on three way. I hadn't talked to him since our break up, which had been eight years by now. When I heard his voice, I was nervous, excited and a little scared. I didn't know how the conversation would go because it had been so long. During our time apart, Tony had two more children, a boy named Elias and a girl named Tia. I knew about Elias because his mother is Meeka, the woman he left me for. I didn't find out about Tia until later on.

After Tony and I spoke on the phone we set up a time to meet at the Marina and talk. We met up a few days later and began talking again. He told me he felt so bad about the way things ended and asked for my forgiveness. I told him I had forgiven him a long time ago. Tony wanted to try again so we started out as friends, just hanging out. I was scared to give him another chance. After all, this man broke my heart and it took a long time for God to heal me. I did not want to go through that again. We talked on the phone almost every day. The more we talked the more I started to have feelings for him again. I wanted to start over and see what would happen. God had blessed me with a state job and I was working at one of the local state prisons. Tony was coming out of a relationship and had moved back in with his mom. He wasn't working, but was trying to get back on his feet. He was still selling dope, but not as much as before. Strangely, I understood because he had a hard time finding a job. Neither one of us ever used crack, so that was the bright side I chose to look at.

We talked about the past and he shared that he wasn't ready to be in a committed relationship at that time. But he was not man enough to tell me. Tony didn't have a car so I had to pick him up when we spent time together. We hung out at MaeD's a lot and he would cook dinner for me after I got off work. It was nice to have him cooking for me again. He was such a good cook. Everything he made tasted as if it was from a restaurant. I loved his gumbo and he made his roo from scratch. It was the best. He could make a meal in a few minutes that would take me hours to prepare. But then again, I was never a good cook. Tony also loved to fish and he would go at least a few times a week with his son Deon. They would come back with bass and there was nothing like eating fresh bass. We would sometimes have fish frys and MaeD and his aunt Ruthie would come over. As I'm writing this, I'm thinking about how good that fish was. I would have potlucks at work and Tony would always cook something. I even remember one of the counselors said that his fried rice tasted better than the restaurant.

Tony would sometimes come to church with me. He was raised Catholic, so he didn't know anything about Christianity. He also didn't like Pastor M at the time, because according to Tony, Pastor M had "pimp-like tendencies". He made me so mad when he said things like that, because I felt like that was an excuse for him not to go to church. I did not tell my Pastors we were in a relationship, because I did not think they would approve. He wasn't a Christian and I thought they would tell me I should not be with him. My Pastors' opinion mattered to me, because they were like parents. I wanted to please them and make them proud of me. Pastor M was my spiritual father. Tony was unemployed, living with his mom, selling dope, and had no car. I knew they were going to say not to be with him. Plus, to make matters worse, Tony didn't come to church regularly.

I went to Tony's house almost every day after work and we spent time together on the weekends. I would stay with him at MaeD's house and it felt good to be there again. It was weird because the boys were teenagers so I had to get to know them again. I say boys because Tony had his biological son Deon and older brother, Alec, whom he raised since he was a year old. I admired the relationship Tony had with his sons. It was nice to see a father being involved in his son's lives even if he couldn't financially be a provider. Tony didn't see his son, Elias because Meeka didn't like the fact that we were a couple again. She was jealous, because she still wanted to be with him. She even told him she wanted to have another baby with him. That hurt my heart, because he really wanted to spend time with Elias. It felt good getting to know Tony again. But I also found out that Tony had been robbed at gunpoint some years back and was pistol whipped. He almost died and had thirty stitches in his head. He had been set up by a close family member.

In addition, Tony was given pain medication after the incident and had become addicted to them. I never saw him take pills, but one night I went to see him and he could hardly hold his spoon to eat. I didn't realize that he was high on pain pills. This was my first time seeing him like that. He would sometimes have seizures which was a side effect of the pills. I still didn't know at that time that he was high on pills. I thought it was him having a seizure from his head injury. I later learned that he went through great lengths to conceal his pill addiction from me. Tony had so many incidents from being high on pain medications.

His aunt Ruthie gave him her truck to use to get around and look for jobs. He was high while driving and clipped two parked cars. I knew all of this and I would ignore the red flags. I wanted things to work so bad this time around. Once again, I dropped another piece of myself. I talked to him about his pill addiction, letting him know my concern, but he would get defensive and say he didn't have a problem. He would tell his family that he was in pain and they would give him the pills. I knew he was addicted. His family would make excuses and it would make me mad. I would tell Ruthie and his uncle Ray that I didn't like Tony going to their houses, because they gave him pills. I would express to them that he had a problem and they weren't helping. I would even beg them to not give him the pills. Yet, they still fed his habit knowing he had to drive home. Sometimes, Tony would wait until he got home to take the pills, but then there were other times when he would drive home high.

But even with knowing Tony had a pill addiction and there had been no positive changes, it didn't stop me from doing what I was about to do next.

Chapter 8

Marriage and Struggles

We dated for four years and decided to get married. There was no elaborate proposal, we just both said we need to get married and that was it. I wish he would have done something to make it special for me. This is where the drama begins...

We wanted to get married in October 2007, but Pastor M asked why couldn't we wait a while. Reluctantly Tony and I waited until January 5, 2008. It was good, because it gave us more time to plan. Tony said that if we didn't get married in January that he was going to call it off, because he didn't want to keep changing the date. He seemed to be in a hurry. We had to watch our budget, because Tony wasn't working. And although I was, we still had to find our own place. I had a coworker who was a wedding planner, so I hired her, and it helped a lot. There were some things I did, but she handled most of the wedding. It was one thing after another coming against us. Tony's niece was supposed to be our flower girl, my godson was supposed to be our ring bearer and MaeD was supposed to pay for our caterer. At the last minute, Tony's niece was a no go because of her mom. I was so irritated, because I had already purchased the dress. My godson's mom told me she couldn't get the outfit for him and I was strapped for cash, so I wasn't able to do it.

To make matters worse, MaeD told us a few weeks before the wedding that she couldn't pay for the catering, but would give us $100. I just felt like she wasn't happy about us getting married. Our relationship changed and she started being distant. I think she was jealous of the relationship and the fact we were getting married. She acted like I was taking her son from her. Tony did everything for her, and I believe she felt like she was losing him. I started questioning if we should get married, because of all the opposition and knowing God gives warning signs. But things, eventually started to come together. Tony's dad, Mr. G, paid for our catering, I was able to have a daughter of one of the sister's from my church and niece as my flower girls. It worked out perfectly, because they already had dresses that were the same as my wedding colors. Pastor M's son was the ring bearer and he took care of the cost. God is good! Tony and I didn't have to pay for a venue, because we were able to have the wedding and reception at our church. I talked to some of the married couples at church and they said that things like this always happen when planning a wedding. This made me feel a little better.

Our wedding day came and went and real life began. The day after our marriage, we stayed home from church and just relaxed. Around 9 that night, Pastor M called and asked if I could bring my tithes to him. Me not thinking anything of it, said sure. I never thought to question why is this man asking me to bring my tithes at 9 pm. Later I thought about it and couldn't help to question, "What was so important that I needed to bring my tithes that late at night, instead of waiting 'until Sunday morning during church?"

Tony was angry to say the least. He was so mad and he didn't want me to go. All I could tell him was that I was doing this unto the Lord, so whatever happens after that is on Pastor M's hands. Pastor M had asked Rhonda for her tithes too. So, I picked them up and took them to his house. I knew there was something wrong with this picture, but I was doing what I thought was right. Looking back, I really thought Tony didn't understand or that he was just making excuses for not wanting to go to church. Now I understand why he was mad.

Anyways, Tony and I started to get settled in our apartment. We were blessed with many wedding gifts, including money. One of the sisters at the church gave us a $50 check. I hadn't had time to deposit it yet. I was going to go deposit the check and realized it was missing. Deon was living with us at the time and Tony tried to blame him saying he must have taken the check. I believed it was Deon, because I didn't think Tony would stoop so low as to take the check when it belonged to the both of us. I looked everywhere for it and couldn't find it. I ended up calling the sister who gave us the check to ask if it had been cashed, and she said yes. She sent me a screenshot of the cashed check and it had been cashed at a check cashing place. I couldn't believe it when I saw the signature on the check was Tony's.

I confronted him about it and he tried to justify what he did by saying it was both of ours. That was the first time I really saw how addicted he was to pain pills. He was strung out enough that he would steal from me or us as he put it. The check belonged to the both of us. It took a while for me to let that go, but I finally did. It was hard to trust Tony, because I didn't know what he would do next. I didn't know how far he would go to get the next high. It was like I was dealing with a dope fiend, but this dope fiend was my husband.

Tony could never keep a job. He would work for about a week and then he would get fired. He either didn't show up, because he was high or he would be high at work and of course that's a liability. But still, the thing about Tony was even though he had his addiction, he was the kindest person with a heart of gold. If someone was in need and he had it, he would give it to them. He was very generous. I loved Tony so much that I wanted to make the marriage work. I suppose it wasn't hard to look past what he was doing, because I wanted to be with him. I loved this man so much. I didn't want this to end, so I dealt with what came along with being with him. Even if it meant sacrificing me.

I was in my late thirties and wanted a baby so bad. I found out I had fibroid tumors so my doctor referred me to a doctor to have them removed. She thought that could be the reason why I wasn't able to get pregnant. I had my surgery and was off work for six weeks. The doctor prescribed pain meds for me, but I hadn't taken them since the surgery. I filled the prescription just in case, but I never thought about using them. I don't remember why I went looking for them, but I found the empty pill bottle and I knew Tony had gotten to them. Once again, he was stealing from me to feed his addiction. I confronted him and he lied as usual. Tony was good at trying to cover his tracks when it came to him getting high. But by now, I was able to determine when he was high by the way he would act or talk. Even if we were talking on the telephone, I was able to hear in his voice if he was high.

With all of this going on, I still wanted to become a mother. I thought I would become pregnant soon after having my surgery, but it didn't happen. My mom even paid for me to go see a fertility specialist who said nothing was wrong with me. When Tony and I were together the first time he never smoked cigarettes but would smoke weed. He was now smoking cigarettes and I asked him to stop. I believe his smoking was decreasing our chances of having a baby, but he had a hard time quitting. I started to get angry, because I wanted a baby so bad and wondered why God hadn't opened my womb. I know Tony's smoking didn't help, but God could do anything He wanted like open my womb. I started to question if had I done something so bad that I didn't deserve it? Was I being punished for marrying Tony and that's not what God wanted for me? I was hurting and crying on the inside, even though laughing on the outside. I had a hard time telling people how I really felt and how this was really painful to me.

People would say, Sister Patrice, when are you going to have kids? I was too embarrassed to tell people that I was struggling. I did share with Sandy, my coworker how I felt and she tried to encourage me. How could someone who had three kids talk to me about having a hard time having kids? Though it was hard, I learned to live with it, because there was nothing else I could do.

Tony would go to either MaeD's, Uncle Ray's or Ruthie's house and they would pay him to do things for them around their house. But they paid him in pain pills. I hated that. It's scary to know that your husband could possibly be driving home under the influence and could hurt himself or someone else. I still continued to ask them not to give him pills but of course they never listened to me. Tony would sometimes take me to work because we only had the one car. He would take Uncle Ray to appointments or go to Ruthie's house to do something. One day he called me at work and told me he was getting pulled over and had an attitude like it was my fault. I was so embarrassed, because I didn't know how I was going to get home. I had previously talked to Sandy about what was going on with us and his addiction. Sandy offered to give me a ride. Tony had said he was on his way walking to my job, so when she was taking me home, we saw him. She picked him up and took us both home. The car had been towed and I had to come up with the money to get it out. Uncle Ray helped us out, because he felt bad since Tony was leaving his house when he got pulled over.

Tony had been speeding and he got pulled over, he also didn't have a license. I know you're asking, why was he driving with no license? He never went to get one and I don't have a reason why I allowed him to drive the car. We were struggling financially, because Tony wasn't working, and everything was on me.

One day I went to dinner with a friend after work and when I came home the apartment was filled with smoke. Tony was on the couch having dozed off from getting high while cooking and it was burning. I thank God I came home when I did, because he could have burned our apartment along with someone else's. I was so mad, I called MaeD to tell her he needed to go back to her. She said that we were married now, and I had to deal with him. I wanted to cuss her out, because she was part of the problem. She was one of the people giving him pills.

In addition, I had been a member of my church for sixteen years, but I felt God leading me to leave. I started attending another ministry, but I was still going to my first church too. I knew the time had come and I had to make a decision to let my first ministry go. I called Pastor M and told him. He asked me what he needed to do to make me stay and I told him, I believed it was time for me to go and he blessed me. He put First Lady M on the phone and she scolded me, condemned me and tried to make me feel guilty. She said God didn't tell me to leave and I didn't hear Him say that. She said if I left it would be detrimental to my marriage and Tony. She was yelling at me and Sandy could hear her and told me to hang up, so I got off the phone. I started to believe I was in a cult and since it was the first church, I had ever been a part of, I didn't realize it until later. It reminded me of when Pastor M asked me to bring my tithes at 9pm the day after my wedding. Tony was mad and there I was the Christian and he was the one seeing in the Spirit. I felt peace and joy about my decision and was looking forward to being a part of this new ministry.

By now, it was 2011. I received a letter stating our rent would be increasing and I couldn't keep up with everything by myself. It was overwhelming. I felt like I had to be the one in control. I told Tony I was going to ask my mom if we could stay with her for a while until we could get on our feet. I talked to her and she said yes. I gave our thirty-day notice to our apartment manager. It was a week before we were supposed to vacate our apartment and my mom called and told me she didn't think it would be a good idea for me and Tony to move in with her. She said she wouldn't be comfortable with Tony staying there, but she said I could. At the time I was hurt, mad, and angry because I didn't know where we were going to live. I didn't know who we could stay with. Tony asked MaeD if we could move in with her, and she said yes. I didn't want to stay there, because everyone in the house smoked cigarettes and I didn't want to smell like it or to have it get in my clothes. But I didn't have a choice and I was grateful she said yes.

So we moved in, but I had a hard time getting comfortable. I didn't want to seem rude, but I didn't want to be around the cigarette smoke so I stayed in my room. MaeD had the boys, Boyd and Lance, whom she had fostered since they were little. They had to be taken care of because they were mentally delayed. She had been in a relationship with a man named Ted for years and he lived there also. Tony and I weren't used to having a lot of people around us. We liked our quiet-ness and they always had visitors. I had to take baths, because the main bathroom only had a bathtub and I had to keep everything in our room. Every day I was taking everything from the bedroom to the bathroom to get ready for work. I finally got somewhat used to this process at MaeD's house. Tony was still on the pills and he had more access now. I wouldn't do laundry at MaeD's house so every Friday after work I would go to the laundromat.

One night I came back from doing our laundry and Tony was really high. MaeD had company; it was Ruthie and an old friend of hers. I was so mad I started crying and the bad part about it was that MaeD didn't see anything wrong with her son being high. She had the nerve to say, "Well at least he's at home and not in the street." It took everything in me to not disrespect her in her home. I just walked off and went in the room. I never involved my mom in my marriage when it came to Tony and his addiction, but I know she knew something was wrong. Maybe that's why she didn't want him to live there. She would sometimes tell me that I could always come home. I believe she didn't want to get involved, but she would have been there if I needed her. I was at my wits end, and I couldn't take it anymore.

In December, 2012, after about four or five months, I told Tony that needed to get our own place. This was not working. I started looking for an apartment again. We looked at a few places, but nothing ever came of them. I was looking in the newspaper and I saw an ad for a condo, so I called the owner. I asked God to please bless us and He did!

Chapter 9

God Had A Plan/God Worked It Out

The owner of the condo, Lu, said we could go look at the condo, so we did. We fell in love with it! It was perfect for us and had everything we needed and wanted. Lu didn't have an application; we just gave her our information on a piece of paper. Tony didn't have credit and mines wasn't the best. I was honest with her. We hadn't heard from her in a few days, so I called her. I told Lu that I knew that my credit wasn't the best, but one thing I always did was pay my rent. She gave us a chance and told us the condo was ours. Tony and I were so excited, we could hardly wait to go. We moved on New Year's Eve.

All we had was our bedroom furniture, kitchen table, and some other little things. We didn't have living room furniture but we didn't care. We were happy to be in our own place and ready for a new start for the new year. Things were going well, and we were getting settled. Tony was still struggling with his addiction, but it seemed like things were better. It was weird, because he would have times when he didn't get high for days and then there would be times when he'd go on binges. I remember being so mad at him when he would be high and telling him I didn't want to come home and find him dead. At the time, I didn't understand the stages of addictions.

It was my birthday, March 6, 2013. Sandy, my co-worker and friend's mom, Sheila, were really good cooks. Sheila cooked everything from scratch so, of course I asked her to make me a full course soul food meal. But Sheila said she wasn't able to make it.

Anyways, my manager called me into her office and said she wanted to take my order for a local restaurant. The restaurant we were ordering from was one of my favorite places. I told my manager what I wanted and went back to my work area. When I got to my office, Sandy and my coworkers had all the food out. Sheila surprised me by making the food I wanted. They also ordered my favorite cake, which is a white cake filled with fresh strawberries and whipped cream frosting. My coworkers bought me gifts. It was one of the best birthdays I've ever had. Growing up, I never had a birthday party, so my desire was and has always been to have a surprise party.

That weekend Tony and I went to San Francisco and walked the Golden Gate Bridge, which was also something I always wanted to do. It made me feel good to have others pouring into me instead of me always pouring into others. I believe at that point, a piece me that I was lacking was finally placed inside of me. A piece of knowing someone cares for me and that I matter.

Tony's birthday was April 2nd and he wanted to go to Los Angeles. We invited my mom to go with us. We also picked up my niece, Nicole and her two year old son, Lil' D. We went to Venice Beach, Santa Monica Pier, and sightseeing in Hollywood. Tony had such a good time and he really enjoyed spending time with Little D. Tony loved kids and he was so good with them. We all enjoyed that weekend and made it back home safely.

About a week later, Tony was complaining of a toothache. I took him to the dentist who of course prescribed pain pills for him to take. I thought to myself, here we go again. I knew it wasn't going to be good, but I hoped it wouldn't be bad. I was so wrong; it was really bad. Tony couldn't wait to fill the prescription and as soon as he got the pills, he called Ruthie. She asked him to bring her some. Truthfully, they would pass out pills like it was candy! It was crazy to me. I got mad and I told Tony not to give her any pills, because the doctor prescribed those to him. Tony didn't understand why I had a problem and we got into a heated argument. I took the pills from him, got in the car, and was getting ready to leave. Tony followed me and kept yelling at me to give him the pills. Since I wouldn't give them to him, he started threatening to break the window and we were going at it for at least ten minutes. It was frightening; things had never got to that point before. I felt like I had no choice. I was mad, but I had to accept it. There was nothing I could do. I don't know why it affected me so much this time. I got tired of arguing, so I just gave in and gave him the pills. I don't think we talked to each other for two days. That didn't surprise me though, because Tony and I would get into arguments over him being on pills and sometimes we would go a day or two without talking . Those were some of the worse times, because I never liked to live with tension. Tony could be so stubborn sometimes when it came to me calling him out on those pills. I would become passive regarding the situation. Tony couldn't understand that he was hurting himself and me.

Addiction is serious and not to be taken lightly. It will make a person say and do things without a second thought. It's a demonic spirit, but it is also an illness. I prayed and fasted for my entire marriage. I desired for Tony to be healed, delivered and set free. I also wanted him to experience God's love and presence in his life. I got so desperate that I told God that even if we didn't stay together, to please deliver him and save his soul. I was willing to sacrifice our marriage so he could be saved. I was tired, discouraged, crying out at home and at church. I didn't know what else to do. I asked God if He heard me? There were times when I would go stay at my mom's house and she never knew because she wouldn't be home. I was exhausted from making excuses for Tony's behavior. I was too embarrassed to let anyone know what was going on. Besides, it wasn't everyone's business, right? Things started to calm down a little bit.

One day Tony and I were in the kitchen and he asked me what was Heaven going to be like. I tried to explain it to him and he said "My mom lied to me." I can't remember what he told me she said. I don't know what made him ask me, but I was happy that he did. It meant he was thinking about life, death, and choices. Tony started reading the bible and would go to church with me more often. He would read Psalm 23 every day and said he didn't understand why he was led to. He even surprised me by going to church by himself on Easter Sunday. I wasn't feeling well. I didn't think he was going to go, but he did. I said to God, "Ok are you doing something?" Tony came with me to a few outreach events at the church. I was so happy to have him there. It looked like God was answering my prayers. But there were still other family issues, we had to cope with.

MaeD and Ruthie were breast cancer survivors and were in remission. When Tony and I stayed with MaeD, she would lay in bed a lot and say she was in pain. We didn't realize that her cancer had come back and with a vengeance. It had spread to her brain so she needed to have surgery. She had the surgery and the doctor removed what he could, but wasn't able to get all of it. But she was doing better and fighting.

Also, Tony and I really wanted a baby and started actively trying. I had even gotten ovulation kits and we were praying God would open my womb. Tony said he had dreams of having a little girl. Some of my coworkers had said they had dreams about me being pregnant. We thought that God was going to do it. We were really excited and believed this was our time. We thought this was a sign. Tony started giving me more compliments and affirmations for no reason. That was one of things I loved about him. No matter how ugly I felt at times, he always knew what to say to make me forget about my feelings about myself.

I worked with two women, Sionce and Krys and they were

talking about going to Disneyland. I hadn't been since I was a little girl. They asked me if I wanted to go and I said yes. It was really last minute for me, but I was excited to go. Krys planned everything and added up the cost to the last penny. The Saturday before we left, Tony had given his life to Christ and completed the New Members class. Sunday, we served as greeters together and he received his certificate for completing the class. The marriage was looking good for us and I was happier than I had been in a long time. Krys, Sionce, and I left the day after Memorial Day and planned to come back home that Friday. We had three day passes and hoppers to go in between Disneyland and California Adventures. I could not wait to get out there. It was the perfect time and perfect weather to go.

We made it to Anaheim and got settled. Afterwards, we went to the park for a little while because it was still early. It was so hot. The first ride we rode was a water ride. I had a small purse and had put my cell phone in the inside not thinking anything of it. We got so soaked on the ride that the inside of my purse got wet. My phone was damaged and I was unable to use it. So, I had no phone for the entire trip. When we got to the room, I used Sionce's phone to call Tony and tell him what happened with my phone. I told him he could call me on

Sionce's phone. I didn't talk to Tony as much, because I didn't want to bug Sionce or Krys by asking to use their phone. I didn't talk to him all day Wednesday.

Wednesday night, Tony called and asked Sionce to have me call him. I called him early Thursday morning and when he answered he sounded like he was high. I was instantly irritated and I didn't really talk. I let him do the talking, but he wasn't talking about anything. I finally told him I had to go, because I was on Sionce's phone and I didn't want to hold her up. He said ok and I was getting ready to hang up, but before I could, he said, "Hello, I love you". I responded and said, "I love you too." But honestly, I really didn't want to, because I was so irritated with him. I almost let it ruin my day and then I said to myself, "Patrice you gotta shake this off!" We all got ready and went to get breakfast. We got to the park and walked around, because we didn't want to ride anything after having just eaten. I suddenly started feeling nauseous. We sat down for a while and I drank some water and it eventually passed. We enjoyed the rest of the day and I didn't talk to Tony for the remainder of the trip.

We left that Friday afternoon and on the way home, Sionce said she had a message on her phone from Tony. She asked me if I wanted her to save it and I said, "No, why would I want you to do that?" We just started laughing. She and Krys both said, you haven't talked to him today and I said yes, I know. So, I called him, but he didn't answer. I didn't think anything of it. We got to my house around 1:30am. I had to use the bathroom bad, so I jumped out the car, ran to the door and started knocking asking Tony to let me in. He didn't answer. I had to run to the car, and get my house key.

I got in the house and ran straight to the bathroom. As I was coming out, I yelled out, "Tony you didn't hear me knocking?" He didn't answer. I said it again. As I was walking towards our room he still didn't answer. He was laying on the bed and I said it one more time. No answer. I said, "Tony, Tony," and no answer.

I thought he was high and had dozed off. Usually when he dozed off it would be hard to wake him. I would have to shake him to wake him up. I touched him and he was cold as ice. He looked like he was sleeping peacefully. The television was on. I guess he was watching TV, fell asleep, and didn't wake up.

I believe he took one too many pills and his heart couldn't take it. I ran out the apartment screaming, "Tony's dead, Tony's dead!" Sionce thought I was playing, and she said, "No he isn't, Stop playing."

I said no, "He's dead!" We walked back into the apartment and she and Krys saw that he was dead. I didn't know what to do. I was in shock, crying, and paralyzed with fear. The first person I called was Pastor J and I thank God he answered as late as it was. I was screaming that Tony was dead and I could barely get anything else out. He told me to call the coroner's office, because since he was gone, there was no need to call the ambulance. It seemed like he and First Lady K got there in minutes. Pastor J called Tony's brother, Jarrod and he and Deon came to the house. Deon came and saw his dad and ran out screaming he wanted to kill someone. Jarrod went in the bedroom, closed the door, and spent time alone with Tony. It was so sad to see. I sat on the couch and screamed. I screamed so hard I peed on myself. Jarrod finally came out. I went back into the room. I yelled, asking Tony to wake up and telling him he was my best friend. What was I going to do without him? Remember I would tell him when he got high that I didn't want to come home and find him dead. Well, that's just what happened. Like Job in the Bible said, "the thing I feared the most has come upon me." (Job 3:25)

The police came to look at Tony's body and they ruled out foul play. I guess that's what they have to do when someone dies in the home. A little while later the coroner came and bagged Tony's body.

I can honestly say that knowing he was in that body bag is an image I will never forget. My mind was all over the place. Neither Tony nor I had life insurance, so now I was stressing over how I was going to pay for his funeral. Stress was outweighing my grief, because I didn't know where I was going to get the money. I really appreciated my Pastors, because they did a go fund me on social media. The bad part about that was some of Tony's family members went on social media saying they don't ask for handouts and I had to remove the post. Yes, the situation was a hot mess!

But, my church family really stepped up during this time and I was so blessed and grateful. The first night I couldn't sleep in the bedroom. I slept in the living room and to be honest, I didn't eat or sleep for three days. We didn't tell MaeD about Tony's death right away. We decided to wait until later that afternoon to give us time to process it and support her together. It was me, Jarrod, Yvette and Ruthie. MaeD was in her bedroom and we went in to tell her. I will never forget her saying, "You mean to tell my son is dead?" All we could do was tell her yes, but that he didn't feel any pain. She was having a hard time, because he died alone. MaeD was supposed to go to our house and help Tony hang pictures. She had cancelled those plans and she felt guilty about that. I was also feeling guilty, because Tony was by himself. I didn't have an autopsy performed on him. Tony died peacefully in his sleep. His doctor said he most likely had a heart attack in his sleep. I was at peace with that and didn't want to investigate any further.

I started to regret having gone to Disneyland and I felt like I should have been there with him. I had guilt when I ate, because my husband was laying in a grave and I was eating good food. Jarrod called their father, Mr. G and said he would pay for the funeral services.

All I could do was thank God! Mr. G said that since I was Tony's wife I should be the one to make all of the arrangements. Things didn't happen that way. Jarrod and his wife, Cheryl made all of the arrangements down to picking out Tony's casket. I was angry about it. That was my husband and none of them were around when we were struggling financially or having issues. Now they want to make all of the decisions concerning his final resting place! There was so much going on even down to who would do the eulogy. Pastor J was our Pastor, so I wanted him to do it. But, Tony's family wanted their aunt, who was also a Pastor, to do it. First Lady K had even asked me to release Pastor J from the services because he was being threatened by Tony's family members. As much as it hurt me, I agreed, but God..

Tony's aunt called me and said she wanted Pastor J to do the eulogy, because he was our Pastor. She said, "Pastors don't step on each other's toes." Tony's family had no choice after that. God worked it out for me. I had friends who said they weren't going to come to Tony's funeral, because there was so much drama. I remember calling Jarrod to tell him that I had given up and they can do what they want. "I'll just show up because I'm tired." I couldn't even grieve for my husband because, there was so much mess going on. I was over it and just wanted this funeral to be over with so I didn't have to deal with them anymore.

One of Tony's family members was supposed to create the slide show, but backed out at the last minute. Thank God I was able to have someone from my church help me.. One of the elders from my previous church worked at a mortuary. She asked the funeral director if she could do Tony's makeup. I wanted to make sure he looked his best and knew she would do it right.

The day came for the viewing. I didn't know how I was going

to get through it, let alone the funeral the next day. There were so many people from Tony's past, his homies, and his brother Jarrod, who was always hyper. It was crazy! A hot mess! It came time to end the viewing and Jarrod wanted him and his homies to take a picture in front of the casket. The funeral director was trying to get them out of there, but they kept taking pictures and talking. It was so frustrating, but they finally left.

My manager at the time came with her husband. She said when she walked to her car there were guys leaning on her car and smoking weed. I was trying to grieve, but there were so many ghetto things going on!

Tony's homies didn't realize that he was no longer that same person from back in the day. He hadn't lived that lifestyle for years, but they were bringing back the past. I was so embarrassed, but what could I do? Jarrod could be ruthless when he wanted to. He had been in and out of prison since he was a teenager and his last stunt made him a three time striker. That meant if he got in trouble again, it was an automatic twenty-five years to life for him. He hadn't gotten in trouble since then, but like the saying goes, you can take the person out the hood, but you can't take the hood out the person. That applies to Jarrod.

It came time for the hardest part which was the funeral. The Pastors picked me up and they had been such a blessing during that time. We got there early. I wanted time to be with Tony alone before anyone else showed up. I stood at the casket staring and talking to him. I wrote him a letter and put a picture of us with it in the casket. I couldn't believe this was final. It was the last time I would see him. I knew it was just a shell, but it was still hard. I walked away from his casket and fell to my knees. Sandy was there and she had to help me up. I couldn't believe I was going through this. Even though Tony took me through a lot emotionally, I loved him and this was hard. Tony's death and attending his funeral was more than one piece leaving me. I felt like a part of me died with him. This was heartbreaking. I had never experienced pain like this before. I didn't know what to do with all this pain.

There were a lot of people at Tony's homegoing. I had a lot of support which I thank God for. They not only prayed for me, but they brought me food and helped me financially. God showed up and I felt loved, which was what I really needed. Even though I lost, I gained. I made it through the services and went to the burial site. I didn't stay long and left before they put Tony in the monument. I went to a small repass for him and then went home. The hard part was knowing that it was final, because Tony had been buried.

The weekend after Tony's homegoing was Father's Day. My nephew and niece, Carbello and Nicole, wanted to surprise their dad by visiting him in Southern California. Nicole was also moving back to Northern California. On the way there, Little D, started pointing and saying, "Uncle Tony." We said, "you see Uncle Tony?" and he said, "Uncle Tony is right there." Little D was only two years old so we knew that he wasn't lying to us. I believe Tony was with us on that car trip. All I could do was cry.

I let Nicole and Little D stay with me until they found an apartment. Three months later they moved out. I had a hard time sleeping by myself and would leave the television on to have some noise. No matter how hard I tried, I just could not sleep. I would be wide awake. I went to see my doctor and she prescribed me sleeping pills. She prescribed two different types, but honestly, neither worked for me.

I was off work for a month. I had good days and bad days, but I pushed my way through no matter what. People would tell me they admired me, because I was so strong and they didn't know how I did it. I told them it was God. If it weren't for the Lord, I don't know how I would have made it through that pain. I understand how people die from a broken heart. My heart was broken. I had to start doing things Tony used to do, like emptying the trash and pumping gas. I no longer had my running buddy with me. I had to get used to doing things by myself. It felt strange and lonely driving in the car by myself. Every time I got in the car, I thought about him.

The first year was really hard. I made sure I went to the cemetery every day no matter what. If I didn't feel like going I made myself go. I would feel guilty if I didn't. I finally had to let it go, because Tony knew I loved him. I just had so much guilt especially when I thought about our last conversation. I thought about how I talked to him and wasn't going to say I love you. If Tony hadn't of said that he loved me first, I wouldn't have said it. It would've eaten me up if he would have died without me saying I love him back. I barely went out and did things, because I felt guilty. Tony was no longer with me. I couldn't do anything, but thank God, because I believe He did everything from Tony becoming a Christian, completing the new members class, to us serving as greeters that Sunday in church. I believe God was preparing Tony to go home to Him. I am so grateful that God didn't allow Tony to go to hell. I started serving a lot at church and I think it was so I could stay busy. When I was busy I didn't have time to think about Tony and grieve. I was happy doing everything and I made a lot of friendships during that season.

I was part of the youth ministry and the kids would call me Momma P. They still call me that to this day. I became a part of the prayer team and did alter calls after Pastor J spoke. I was right in my element with prayer. I grew a lot during that time and learned a lot about myself. I now know that my love language is attention, affection, affirmation and quality time. I like to receive gifts, but I would rather spend time with the man I love. Tony gave all of that to me. Even down to his final months and with all of the struggles and hard times, I know he loved me.

Before Tony died, I had reconnected with a sister from my first church, named Rashaun. We had started messaging each other on Facebook and when Tony died she reached out to me. She couldn't believe it, because we had been talking to each other about me having a baby. After Tony died, Rashaun and I got really close. We called and texted a lot.

She told me things that I know only God spoke to her about.

Things that no one knew but God, Tony, and I. It was scary to hear, but it was a comfort at the same time. I know it was God who revealed those things to her. I donated Tony's clothes to the mission's ministry for Thanksgiving, 2014. I cried and it was hard, but God got me through it. I kept a few of his items. I took my wedding rings off and put them on a necklace to wear. But after a while, I stopped wearing it, and packed them away. Slowly I was letting go and dealing with my life as a widow. It wasn't easy, but I was getting through it. By now, a few years had gone by and it was 2015. One of my uncles on my Father's side, named Buster died and I wanted to go to the homegoing. He lived in my hometown of Pittsburg, California. I hadn't been a part of my relatives lives on my Father's side, but I wanted to show my respect. One of my cousin's, Norma, was going to be there. She lived in San Diego, but we kept in touch over the years. I went to the homegoing not knowing what would happen next.

Norma introduced me to my brother, Kevin and his mother Anita, whom I never got to meet because they didn't come to my father's homegoing. I cried and hugged him. I couldn't believe he was in his twenties, the same age as my niece Nicole. I couldn't believe this was my first time seeing him. I felt kind of jealous, because they had been with my father when he died. Kevin had more time with him than Monique and I ever had. There was nothing else to really say to Anita. She said I was welcomed to come see her anytime I wanted to, but I knew that would never happen. This is the woman who didn't want my dad to see me before he died. It was her fault that I couldn't say my final goodbye to him when he was alive. But it's now over and done with and I have forgiven her because I can't change the past. How can I not forgive someone and expect God to forgive me for all that I have done?

Kevin gave me his number and I really wanted to get to know him, but when I called the number was disconnected. To this day, I haven't seen or talked to him since. I tried to look him up on social media, but wasn't able to find him. Maybe God didn't want that connection to happen and I'm okay with that. If it was or is meant to happen, it will happen.

The following year, in 2016, my landlord told me I had to move out because, she needed to move her dad into the condo. So, I said, "Ok Lord, what am I supposed to do now?" Moving again! I'd been thinking of relocating and I thought about Texas, but I wasn't sure. I then started thinking about Georgia. My friend from church, Sherri's son, Don had recently moved out there. She had been out there the year before and said it was nice. Wendy and I had talked about going to Atlanta years ago, but life got in the way and we never went. I knew I needed a change so I talked to my Pastors about it. They said they would pray for me. I talked to Sherri and she said Don said we could stay with him when we came out there. I asked my mom if I could stay with her to save money to relocate. She said yes and that she would make room for me. But I ended up sleeping on the couch, because Monique and her children, Carballo, Nicole and Little D were all living there.

The house was crowded, and it was a major adjustment. I put all of my things in storage and my clothes were in totes in the main closet of the house. I had no privacy, but I had a roof over my head and I was grateful for that. I did have a hard time because I had to adjust to everyone else. I was saving money, but I was helping out at the same time. Sherri and I went to Atlanta in June of 2016. I wanted to visit and scope it out to see if this was where I wanted to live. We stayed with her son, Don and we had so much fun. I needed that trip. We did so much sightseeing and every day we were doing something. I made the decision during that trip that I was going to try Atlanta. I started looking into relocating out there. I talked to Sherri about possibly moving in with Don until I could find my own place, but I never got up the nerve to ask him. I found out that one of the sisters from my first church, named Brean lived out there. I called her and asked if I could stay with her until I could get a place. She said yes and that she wouldn't charge me rent. I explained to her that I would have to pay her something. We discussed me coming out there after Christmas. She said that would be perfect, because she was moving into her new apartment in November.

It was official, I was moving to Atlanta, Georgia. I was excited, scared and nervous all at once. I had never lived outside of California let alone away from all of my family. I didn't have family out there and the only people I knew were Don, Brean and someone I knew from high school named Star. I told everyone that I was moving and some people didn't believe me, but they soon found out I wasn't playing. I saved up as much money as I could and cashed out my vacation time at my state job. I was able to pay off my car. I sold some of the items from my storage and gave things away. My mom was leery about me leaving, but she said I was an adult and wanted me to be happy.

Before moving, I looked for jobs, but I had no idea how widespread Georgia was. So, I decided to wait until I actually got out there. I planned to drive my car, but I needed someone to drive with me. My sis and my girl, Lizette from church said she would drive with me. I couldn't believe I was really getting ready to do this. I got scared, had mixed feelings and started questioning myself. What was wrong with me? Was I ready to do this? Was I able to do this? But the scrip-ture, "I can do all things through Christ who gives me strength." (Phil 4:13), came to me.

I spent time with family and friends before I left. Christmas Day was bittersweet, because I was leaving the day after. I got up the next day with the car packed to the max. I only took clothes and important things. I had to pick Lizette up, so I said my goodbyes to my family, and I was off. I got to Lizette's house and we said our goodbyes there. Here's where my new journey began...

Chapter 10

Fresh Start

On the first day of driving to Atlanta we were in Arizona on the highway and it was dark. Lizette was driving and we hit some black ice. We decided it would be best to get a room for the night and start fresh the next day. We got up early the next day and we drove twenty-four hours straight and finally made it to Atlanta. We were so tired I think we must have slept almost twenty-four hours. I couldn't believe I was in another state starting over. I was nervous. What did I just do? I had literally left everything familiar to me, family, job, church, friends and moved to this unfamiliar place where I didn't know anyone except for a few people.

Even though Brean and I had went to church together, I didn't know her that well. I was nervous about being there, but excited for this new beginning. I knew when I came that I wouldn't have my own bedroom, because Brean wanted to get foster kids which is what she had done for years. At first, she said she was going to wait awhile, because she didn't have time with work. But about a week after I got there, she got one teenage girl. Brean worked and two of her sons had come from California to live. One of them named Rick, shared an apartment with someone in the same complex. Her other son, Ronnie was back and forth between Brean and Rick's house. That didn't last long, because the next thing I knew they both were constantly coming to the house. They would come early in the morning and would stay all day.

By this time, I was no longer in the bedroom, but I was sleeping on Brean's pull out couch in the living room. The foster child was a teenage girl and she had the bedroom. Brean ended up getting another foster girl. They had the bedroom and I had to share a closet with them. I was uncomfortable because not only did I not have any privacy, but I had to share a closet with these girls I didn't know. They weren't the cleanest nor the neatest either. I wasn't working at the time, but I was looking so I had to take them with me to interviews. Brean didn't want them staying in the house with Rick and Ronnie who were in their early twenties. Brean worked from 5:30am to 1:30pm and she would some-times come home and cook.

We started sharing the cooking responsibilities while I wasn't working. Even though she said I didn't have to pay her rent, I told her

I would help with groceries and take over one of her bills. I took over the cable bill. I also bought things that I saw she needed like cleaning supplies. I bought my own laundry soap and personal hygiene things. I started getting irritated, because I was tired of not having privacy and it was hard for me to get comfortable. I didn't know when Rick or Ronnie would show up and they would come at all times of the day and night.

I finally got a job in March and I was working every day except for Sunday. I was working ten hour shifts and would leave at 4:30am and wouldn't get home until after 6pm. I was hardly at Brean's house so I hardly ate there in the evening, unless she cooked and saved me something. Most of the time there would be nothing left, because between Brean, the foster girls, and her sons, they would eat everything. Brean finally started putting a plate to the side for me. I would help her in any way I was able to, but she always seemed to need help financially. It started out with me helping her out financially with $150. I understand that people sometimes have hard times but it went from that to her saying she forgot to pay her car note and another bill, so she asked me for $700.

I also, took care of the foster girls most of the time. I would make sure they ate dinner, because sometimes Brean would come home and say she had already eaten. This left the girls having to figure out dinner for themselves. But these girls knew nothing about cooking. They barely kept themselves clean and lacked adequate hygiene skills. I would have to make sure they took showers, because they would just put clothes and perfume on. I only hoped to have stayed with Brean for three months. But when that third month came, I had just gotten a full time job, so that caused me to stay longer.

So, there I was taking care of her foster children, picking up the slack of her bills (even when she mismanaged her money), and having no privacy for myself. Moving out was confirmed when she asked me to start paying another bill. I felt like I couldn't say no, because I had nowhere to go; no family or friends so I had no choice. This is when I really started feeling like I was being taken advantage of. Another piece falling off of me. A piece of me being taken advantage of.

I had money to move and get things I needed for my new place, but Brean was draining me of that. If I didn't do something soon, I wasn't going to have enough money to move. I started feeling like I had made a mistake, but I also believed that it wasn't meant for me to go back to California.

As the reader, I'm sure you have noticed that I don't give up easily no matter what I'm faced with. I knew it was time for me to start looking for my own place. I started looking for a place closer to where my job was, because my commute was almost two hours. I asked coworkers if they knew of any apartments in a safe neighborhood, because I wasn't familiar with the area. One of my co-workers told me about an apartment complex he once lived in. Brean was going to California for a week and was taking the foster girls with her. This was my chance to have some peace and quiet. Not to mention, really try to find a place.

One day I went to an apartment complex in Roswell to check it out. I applied for a one bedroom and got approved! Thank you Jesus!! I paid my rent for the next two months and bought living room and bedroom furniture. I was so excited. This is going to be a blessing. Or so I thought. I didn't tell Brean I was moving, because I wanted to wait until she got back to Atlanta. So, when she got back, I let her know I was moving. I moved out of Brean's house that same week. It felt so good to have my own place after sleeping on couches for over a year. I was sleeping on a brand new mattress. Honestly, I didn't know how to act! I was still working and the job was going ok. It was a temporary position that eventually became permanent, but I was working so much that I couldn't do anything else. The only day I had off work was Sunday. I was a member of a church that I had joined when I first moved to Atlanta and I was growing spiritually. My relationship with God was closer than it had ever been. I was on the Prayer Team and I was really fulfilled there. The Pastor's sermons were always on point and he was like a walking bible.

I was ready to leave my current job, because not only was I working too much, but the pay was low. I thought I would have been given a raise when I became permanent, but that didn't happen. I needed to make more money. This is when I found out that Georgia doesn't pay well. I stepped out on faith and quit that job. I had money saved up so I was able to handle my bills for a few months. As time went on, I started panicking, because I had a hard time finding another job. I started to think I had made a mistake. But God! I applied for this company to work in the medical field and I was offered the job. I was out of work for two months, but I finally started my new job right after Thanksgiving 2017. God had given me favor.

I started seeing roaches in my house and I wasn't used to that.

I had never lived in a house with them before and I wasn't about to start now. I know people say there are a lot of bugs in the south, but I didn't want to see them in my house. I didn't know where they were coming from so the apartment manager would have pest control come out once a week to monitor my apartment. I still had them. I wasn't able to sleep at night and I always had to have a light or the television on when I slept. I couldn't take it anymore and I finally asked to transfer to another apartment. The manager agreed. Things went from bad to worse. I lived on the second floor and there was someone above me who had no consideration for people below. He would make all kinds of noise and have parties. I also had the same issue with roaches in that place. I had to call the police on my upstairs neighbor numerous times. The manager had also gotten complaints from other tenants about the noise. The manager finally started the eviction process on that tenant and he was finally evicted.

I was finished with that problem, but still had the roach issue. I couldn't get comfortable. I was so tired of living like that. I wasn't a dirty person nor did I have a lot of things in my apartment. That apartment was no better than the first one. I wanted to move, but by the time I was ready to look, I had to wait another year or break my lease. I decided to wait it out. The job was going good, but I still needed to make more money. I was starting to struggle and I couldn't keep up with everything. I was starting to drown with all of my bills. I was sinking more and more and finally I had to reach out for help.

My job had a program where they help employees who are having a hard time paying rent and utilities. I was able to get help one month from them. I was overdrawn a few thousand dollars in my account and I had no money to pay it back. Things were getting worse, because I couldn't catch up. There were some other programs that I went to and they also helped me.

Sandy, my friend and co-worker from California whom I mentioned earlier, helped me financially. I was able to get caught up with my bills. I really appreciated her because I was on the verge of possibly being evicted. I was grateful to her and God for helping me through those hard times. There was a time when my gas and electricity got caught off but, God always made a way to get it turned back on immediately.

Eventually, I decided I had to get a second job in May of 2018, because I couldn't survive with just one. By this time, I had gotten a new job with the same company. I also started working for a cleaning service Monday through Friday from 5pm until 8 or 8:30pm. It didn't pay much and when I added the money versus the labor of bending and stooping so much, it wasn't worth it. I put in my notice and instead, I started driving for Uber Eats. I was able to make my own hours. I would drive a few hours after work and mostly all day on Saturday. I was learning my way around my city and other surrounding cities.

The two things I didn't like about it was that it wasn't consistent money and when the weather was bad, I didn't want to drive. Also, it was a lot of wear and tear on my car. I started looking for a different part time job, but I couldn't find anything with the hours I needed. In March of 2019, I found a job doing data entry for a company who processed retainers, braces, and other dental products. The only thing is that it was full time and it was Monday through Friday 4pm-12am. I took it, because I needed the money. It was brutal and I was so tired and struggling. But I forced myself to do it, because I needed to pay my bills. I would get home around 12:30am, get to bed and be up at 4:30am to go to my first job. But I worked it out.

Suddenly I wasn't feeling well. I didn't know what was wrong. I would be overly tired, but I thought it was because of working two full time jobs. I also wasn't sleeping at night and I would wake up drenched in sweat. My clothes would feel like I jumped in a swimming pool. I would sleep with my air conditioner and fan on and I would still wake up in a cold sweat. I was vomiting occasionally in the mornings when I would get ready for work and had dizziness and nausea. I thought I was going through peri menopause because of my symptoms. It had gotten to the point where I couldn't handle it anymore so I went to the ER. The doctor said I was dehydrated and gave me an IV and some medicine for the nausea.

A few days later I still wasn't feeling well, so I made an appointment with my primary care doctor. I explained to him my symp-toms and he examined me and he said he thought I might have a hyperactive thyroid. I had no idea what this diagnosis was, but I was happy in a way. I was happy, because I now knew something was wrong and I wasn't crazy. I had been sick for over three months and had no idea what was wrong until then. He sent me to have lab work done to confirm and that's what it was. I was diagnosed in June 2019 with a hyperactive thyroid. Although I was still working two jobs, I was looking for another job.

This time, I applied for a work-from- home job and I got it. I was able to quit my second job for the work-from-home job, but I still wasn't feeling good. So, my doctor took me off work for two weeks. He thought it would give the medication time to get into my system. The medicine was making me feel better and I was relieved. I was working my two jobs and even though this job was working-from-home it was still full time and long hours. I worked 3:15pm-11pm Sunday through Thursday. I really wanted to be off from both jobs on the weekend, so I talked to my manager about it. When a slot became available, he gave it to me. I was excited about having the weekends off. I felt like I could go out and do things I wanted to do.

I was still dealing with the roach situation and decided to look for another place. I was determined to move and not sign another lease. It was like I was dealing with a slum lord and I was tired of having issues and feeling like they weren't doing anything. I saw an ad for an apartment by a private owner, Jo. I emailed her and she had me come over and look at it. It was already furnished, but I had my own furniture. I asked Jo if that would be a deal breaker. I wasn't even sure I would get it, but I really liked it. Jo called and offered the apartment to me. She let me bring my furniture from my house and I moved in a few weeks before my lease was up at my other apartment. I'll never forget what Jo said to me when I went to her house to sign the lease.

She said, "God told me to give you this apartment." I knew that she wasn't lying, because God knew I needed to leave from where I was at. She had other people who were interested in the apartment, but God told her no. Rent to His daughter, Patrice. But God!! That was October, 2019.

I became a member of yet another church and I couldn't figure out where God wanted me to serve. I tried a few things, but felt like it wasn't where I was supposed to be. I didn't want to serve just to do something. My heart has been and still is with praying. I became part of a life group at my current church in, which I am still a part of.

With COVID-19 in 2020, we weren't able to get together. Myself and two of the ladies, Antionette and Jenean, decided to have prayer calls three days a week where we each have a day that we pray and fast. I invited Wendy to be a part of it too. We sometimes have bible study on certain topics. This has been a blessing to me, because I've grown to love these ladies and they are like sisters to me. We laugh, cry, pray and encourage each other. I love that we can be honest and transparent with one another.

I'm at a point in my life now where I want to change my career field so I've been going to school. I'm still working two full time jobs.

My thyroid condition is under control and I'm so grateful for where I am today.

With everything I've learned, I would say to you. No matter what life may throw at you, keep going and don't stop. It may get hard sometimes, but just know that you're stronger than you may think. Trouble won't last always and seasons change so you won't stay in your predicament forever. God's got you and you can get through anything with Him. Also, know your worth. Don't continue to pour into people to the point where you're left empty with nothing left to give. Don't love someone and give your all without it being reciprocated. If people cannot love and give you what you need, think about if it's worth it to stay in the relationship. You should not be the only one giving and not receiving in return. Don't help someone who doesn't want to help themselves. You don't want to become an enabler to people. Don't settle!

You deserve to be loved, appreciated, and respected. And don't give up, because there is someone out there who will give you what you need and deserve. Believe me. It's worth the wait. I'm single and never did have the child I desired. It hurts sometimes, but I'm okay with it. I no longer hurt as much as I used to over Tony's death. God has blessed me and He takes good care of me. I'm still a work in progress, but He is putting me back together PIECE BY PIECE.....

About the Author

Patrice was raised in Suisun, California before she relocated to Georgia in 2016. She has experienced losses in her life that have shaped her into the woman she is today. Patrice grew up without her father in her life and that was her first experience of rejection at an early age.

Patrice obtained her Associates degree in Business through Heald Business College in 2003. She later began her career with the State of California in 2003. She was in a relationship with her first love who ended up breaking her heart. They reconnected in 2004 and in spite of their struggles, were married in 2008. Patrice writes about how she endured the hardships in her marriage and how God turned it around for good. She became a widow when her husband died suddenly in 2013.

Patrice continued to work for the State of California until she resigned in 2016 to relocate to Georgia. She is currently working as an out-patient surgery scheduler while working on obtaining her certification in medical coding and billing. She hopes to establish herself as her own contractor in medical coding and billing.

Patrice also hopes to write another book on Prayer. She would like the women who read her book to be ministered to, receive healing and to realize their worth. One of her favorite scriptures is, **"Now unto Him who is able to do exceedingly abundantly above all that we ask or think, according to the power that worketh in us. "(Ephesians 3:20).**

Made in the USA
Monee, IL
19 July 2021